The Winning Resume 2nd Ed.

Get Hired Today with These Groundbreaking Resume Secre~

Steve Williams

ii

CONTENTS

INTRODUCTION

Resumes are a very tricky thing to create. On one hand they can be an extremely powerful tool that can be used to impress a potential employer as well as showcase all of your best achievements. On the other hand when done incorrectly a resume can do the exact opposite. It can ruin your chances at getting a job in which you are completely qualified for simply by being formatted and created wrong.

After reading this book you will understand how to create a resume that will get you interviews. I will cover everything from what an employer looks for in a resume, actually creating your resume, how to create a good cover letter, and much more. Inside the book we will dissect each part of the resume and explain the good and the bad about each part as well as what can be done to minimize any shortcomings you might have.

I want to thank you again for purchasing this book and I sincerely hope that you will be able to benefit from it and accomplish your career goals. Changing careers can be tough, but with the knowledge you gain from this book it should be much easier!

THANK YOU FOR BUYING THIS PINNACLE PUBLISHERS BOOK!

Join our mailing list and get updates on new releases, deals, bonus content and other great books from Pinnacle Publishers. We also give away a new eBook every week completely free!

Scan the Above QR Code to Sign Up

Or visit us online to sign up at
www.pinnaclepublish.com/newsletter

Chapter 1 - Focus on Importance

Having a well thought out resume is very important and most of us know that, but the problem is that writing a resume is not something we do on a regular basis. Most people don't even look at their resume for years at a time, not until they need or want to find a new job. Most of us know how to create a basic resume. We know that we should list our work experience, the positions we have held, volunteer work, and special recognitions, but many people forget about strategy when it comes to resume writing.

Instead of writing the resume for the reader, it is written for the person who is writing it, which is a huge mistake. The resume has to be written for the reader, which means you need to focus on the things that are important when preparing to write your resume.

When we are taught how to write a resume in high school, we are told that we should include all of our clubs, groups, awards, and work experience. 35 years later, potential employers don't care so much about all of that information.

You have to keep your resume up-to-date, but it does not need to include everything there is to know about you. When you are sitting down and deciding what you are going to put in your resume, you need to first understand that it is best if you only have one page if possible. This means that you need to avoid putting in unimportant information. This includes high school grade point average, high school sports, high school anything, as well as your appearance, what your first job was (it does not matter that you work at Mc Donald's the summer you turned 16) and so on.

Of course, these all have an emotional value to you as the writer. They will always be accomplishments that you are proud of but remember, you are writing a resume for the potential employer, not for yourself.

So who is going to be looking at your resume? The first person who is going to read your resume is going to be the business secretary, then it will move on to HR or a recruiting manager, who will decide if you are a potential candidate. Those are the first two steps your resume has to get through before you can get called in for an interview. Once you have the interview, the resume does not matter as much, but if your resume does not make it through the first two steps of the process, you will not get an interview and you will not get the job.

You need to emotionally detach yourself from the resume. It may feel good to put all of that information on a piece of paper, look at it, and say, "Look what I have accomplished," but that is not what is important to the reader. If you want to make a list of your accomplishments, by all means, do so, but on a separate piece of paper.

If you find that you are putting some type of information down on the resume, hoping that it will grab the reader's attention, you need to ask yourself if the information is important or if you are putting that information on there to make you feel good. If you are worried that the resume is full of irrelevant information, the best thing you can do is hire a professional to go over it with you.

The reader also wants to see the information in a specific order, which would be reverse chronological. Of course, many of us were taught that our resumes should be in chronological order, but the fact is that the reader wants to see the most recent information first. As I stated previously, the fact that you worked in fast food when you were 16 means nothing when compared to the most recent place you have worked.

Listing your information in chronological order could very well cost you the opportunity you have been looking for. Remember, people do not have huge attention spans, there is just too much to get done so you want to place the most impressive information (i.e., your last job) at the top of the page so you can guarantee the potential employer has a chance to look at it before becoming distracted or losing interest.

You also need to understand that your reader is not dumb and you cannot try to hide huge gaps of unemployment in your resume. They will not go unnoticed. Instead, make sure that you provide information about that time period. Also, do not try to use flashy words such as "avant-garde" thinker. You may think that it makes you look smarter, but it is going to get nothing more than an eye roll from the reader. Stay professional, but conservative at the same time. You don't want the potential employer thinking that you are the type of person who tries to show others up.

You need to understand that today, you are going to be competing with a ton of other people and it is not the reader's intention to include your resume in the small pile of potential hires but to exclude it. This means that they will be looking for any reason that you would not be a good fit with the company or that you would be a risky hire. For this reason, you need to make sure that you are only including relevant information and that you do not look as if you are trying to build yourself up. Ask yourself, "If I were looking to hire someone, would I consider someone with my resume?"

When it comes to providing relevant information for the reader, what it all boils down to is knowing what the reader will be looking for. If you are applying for an office job, there is no need to go into a lot of detail about the daycare you worked out. Just list the irrelevant jobs and give more detail about the relevant ones, or give details about the job duties you were responsible for that pertain to the job you are applying to.

To finish up this chapter, I want to make sure that you understand that you may need more than one resume if you are applying for jobs in different areas. Make sure that your resume is focused on that particular area and that you write a separate resume for each field you will be applying in.

STEVE WILLIAMS

Chapter 2 - Make Your Resume Stand Out

You shouldn't go out and purchase sweet smelling paper with pretty flowers around the edges to make your resume stand out. That type of resume only looks like it was made by a high school girl and will get thrown out quickly.

Instead, you need to make sure that your resume stands out to your potential employer by following the guidelines I will give you in this chapter. The first thing that you need to do to make sure that your resume stands out is to make sure it does not stand out. Yes, you read that right.

I stated in the previous chapter that the first thing potential employers are going to do is to look for a reason to throw out resumes. The way that they do this is by scanning for obvious errors. Errors such as spelling, grammar, or even typos will get your resume thrown out quickly so take the time to make sure that your resume does not stand out to the person who is doing the scanning. You also want to make sure that your resume follows the proper format and includes all of the necessary information or it will be one of the first thrown into the trash.

For each job available, there are literally over a hundred applicants, which means potential employers have a huge pool of applicants to choose from and they are not going to settle for someone who will settle for mistakes on their resume.

The next thing you want to do to make sure that your resume stands out is to make sure that you use important key words. One way to find out what these words are is to carefully read the job posting, talk to a friend who is employed by the company, or search for information about your targeted job title.

You also want to ensure that you send your resume to the right person and a few others as well. You always want to send the resume to the person who is listed in the job post, but you can take it a step further by locating the hiring managers' email address, and anyone else in the company who might be interested in your resume. This will ensure that if your resume is looked over for some reason, there will be more sets of eyes on it and that will increase your chances of getting an interview.

While you are creating your resume, you want to remember that you are not using the resume to get the job. Instead, you are using the resume to get an interview and then it will be up to you to get the job yourself so leave out all of the personal information such as "I'm a happy person who loves to work and gets along with everyone". Not only does this look like you are trying too hard, but this is also stuff that you want to shine through your personality when you do get the interview. The resume should be nothing more than facts.

You also want to ensure that your resume is clean and easy to read. This means that you do not want huge blocks of text. Think about it like this, when you are reading on social media and the text is a huge block with no spaces between the paragraphs, how much of it do you actually read?

I will be honest, I tend to skip over the majority of the text and if nothing catches my eye, I ignore it completely. That is exactly what the reader is going to do when it comes to your resume. Instead of having huge blocks of text, break it up by using paragraphs and bullet points.

You don't want to get too creative with your resume format. Remember, you want your resume to stand out, but not if that means that it will get tossed out. When in doubt, just stick with the standard settings on your computer and keep things simple.

When you are saving your resume to your computer, you want to make sure that the name is distinctive. For example, JohnDoe_projectmanager.docx (.doc, .pdf, or whatever format you want to use) would be a great name. What you do not want to do is name it something like-momsresume.doc or resume.pdf.

The reason for this is that many of our resumes are sent digitally as an attachment to an email. If the name of the file does not stand out, chances are, your resume will not even be looked at.

Bonus Tip- Keep track of which resume you send to each company. As I stated in the previous chapter, you will want to create a few different resumes, one for each field you will be applying in. When you are doing this, it is important to make sure that you are organized from the start by keeping track of which resume you sent to which company because sending the wrong resumes to a company or forgetting which one you sent to which company could cost you a job. This is another reason you want to name them distinctively. You will never remember what resume1, resume2, and resume3 are, but by using your name as well as the field that the specific resume is for, you will never have to worry about sending the wrong resume.

Most resume templates are going to have an area for you to place your objective as well as a summary. Most of the time, you can completely fail at the summary and the objective and still get the job so I suggest that you don't even include them. This is just space that is being taken up by irrelevant information that could be used to convey something of more importance.

Remember, you are trying to keep this to one page and to do so, you will need to cut out all irrelevant information, including the summary and objective.

Your education is going to be important when it comes to getting a job when you are fresh out of college. This is the time that you should list your GPA, the groups and clubs you were part of as well as any awards. After you have had a few years of work experience, this information is not as relevant, but when you are starting out, you want to make your resume stand out as much as possible and you will want to include all of your accomplishments.

Let the numbers speak for you. When you are listing your responsibilities for one specific job, be as specific as you possibly can. For example, instead of saying "Responsible for training new employees", say "Trained 17 new employees on safety standards." You can also list items such as "Raised employee moral by implementing a company newsletter featuring employees". Include anything that you did that saved the company money, improved the work place, or helped others. If you have the numbers, include them.

There are times when numbers can hurt you though. One example of this might be that you figured out a better way to make a product, saving the company over a million dollars. Of course, that sounds amazing but you don't want to oversell yourself. Instead, you could say "Implemented a new way to create said product, which saved the company time and money".

This way, you do not sound as if you are bragging, but you are showing that you are innovative and creative. You do want to make sure that you are only using the information that is relevant to the job you are applying for. It may be impressive that you were in charge of the company book club, at least it may be impressive to you, but it may not be that important for a potential employer.

When you are creating your resume, you need to use as few acronyms as possible. These are used in most workplaces, but that does not mean that their meaning will carry over to another workplace. For example, at the job I used to have, we used ICVPCKCHR, which stood for Integrity, Compliance, Valued Creation, Principled Entrepreneurship, Customer focus, Knowledge, Change... and so on.

No one else would ever know what that is, so there would be no reason for me to share that acronym. But those are good words to put into your resume if you are lacking some.

Hobbies are the next area that you will want to look at. So many people are ready and willing to talk about their hobbies, dedicating an entire paragraph to what they enjoy doing when they are not at work. It is great for you to share your hobbies if they pertain to what you do at work or that helps you stand out. You don't have to include that you love to dig in your flower garden, but if you run the local soup kitchen, this will show that you have management skills (provided the kitchen is a success).

Chapter 3 - Down to Details

Now that you know how to create your resume and what to include in it, we need to focus on the details. Details are important, especially when it comes to resume writing.

The first detail you need to focus on is ensuring that all of the most important information is right up front. I stated earlier that most people are going to glance through your resume when it arrives at the company and if they are not able to find the important information, you are not going to get an interview. Make sure they have what they need at the beginning of the resume.

Typography is the next detail you want to focus on. You always want to make sure that your font is not too big or too small (which is the worst of the two). It is recommended that you stay with an 11 or 12 point font when you are typing up a professional document.

Stick with Arial and Times for your fonts. We all know that there are some beautiful fonts out there and would love to play with them to make our documents beautiful, but a resume is not the place to do this. Instead, stick with the basics when typing your resume.

Make sure that you are not using text talk when you are typing up your resume. This may seem like a silly tip to give but trust me, it happens and many LOL's end up on resumes as well. Just don't do it. This includes typing in all CAPS.

It is understandable that you want to draw the reader's attention to what you are saying, but this is why we have options such as **bold,** *italics*, and <u>underline.</u> While we are on the topic of underline, don't get too creative there either. No manager wants to see this mess when they are trying to read through a resume.

Don't use highlighting too much either, or ever, if you can help it and don't change the color of your font. There is nothing more blinding than a resume of many colors. This type of stuff may look pretty and seem creative to you, but to your potential employer, it is excessive and annoying.

Don't include the 'Captain Obvious' information such as available for an interview or references available. You see, if you are sending your resume to a company, they already know that you are available for an interview and that you will provide them with references. Avoid any information that makes the reader think, "Thank you, Captain Obvious."

One of the great things about a resume is that it does not have to be perfectly even document, meaning you don't have to dedicate 200 words to each job. If there is one job that highlights your skills more than another, you are free to add more detail under that job and less under the one that does not highlight your skills.

You can also throw in some of your big name clients as long as you did not sign a confidentiality agreement. It may seem a bit tactless, but some managers will be more likely to hire you if they know you have worked for someone with a big name.

It is possible that this can hurt you as well. In my field, I have worked for several big name people who will remain nameless. Telling my future clients this will help me to get more jobs, but if I were to go out and apply for a job with a company, I don't think it would do me any good. This is because we all know there are people out there who make up insanely wild stories about who they have worked for and you don't want to be that person.

So the best thing I have found is that you can drop one big name per field and that person needs to be relevant to that field of work. Any more than one name and it looks like you are making up stories.

Self-employed vs. working in a traditional environment is important as well. On one hand, being self-employed is going to show that you are motivated and an entrepreneur, but you are also going to have to show the potential employer that you can work well with others and that you are capable of working in a traditional work environment. Employers do not look down on self-employment at all but you should expect that they will ask you plenty of questions about it during the interview.

This is because many people who have large gaps in their resumes fill them with a self-employed section, when, in fact, they were not employed at all. Don't lie about this on your resume because they will ask the hard questions and they will know if you were making it up. That will cost you the job.

Keep it positive. You do not need to include the things you hated about your last job or why you are leaving. You will be asked that in your interview and even then, you want to keep it as positive as possible. If you feel negatively about your previous jobs, you just need to keep it to yourself because employers will think that eventually, you will begin feeling the same way about their workplace. This is especially important if you have a history of feeling negatively about your previous employers.

Don't include a picture. Of course, you are beautiful, but unless you are applying for a job where your looks actually matter, such as a modeling job or acting job, your potential employer will not need a picture of you. They will see you soon enough when you come in for an interview so leave the pictures off and fill that space with important information.

Identify the possible problems that the employer might be facing and then list the relevant information on your resume. For example, if the company you are wanting to work for has a history of low employee moral or a high turnover rate, make sure that you focus on your skills that can be utilized when handling those issues. This will give you an upper hand against all of the other applicants.

Remember that you are trying to sell yourself to the potential employer and you need to make sure you mention everything that is of importance. One example of this might be that at 16, you sold hamburgers. This is not important information, but if you are applying for a management position and you were promoted to manager at the age of 16 where you sold those hamburgers, that is important to mention. Of course, you don't have to mention every single accomplishment and should focus on the larger accomplishments.

Discrimination is against the law…if you can prove it, but if you list a bunch of information that is irrelevant on your resume, it is up to management if they want to call you in or not for an interview.

This type of information might be your political views (right or left), religious views (even if you need specific days off, wait until you have a job offer to discuss this) age, and even sexual orientation. If you have some type of disability, wait to discuss this as well. You want the potential employer to meet you before you ever begin talking about any of this if you talk about it at all.

Keep the salary you are asking for in mind while you are creating your resume. If you want 150,000 dollars a year, then your resume needs to reflect that you deserve that amount of money. If your resume does not reflect that you do deserve the amount you are asking for, or that the job pays, you are not going to get called into an interview. Make sure you proofread, edit, proofread, double check, and then have a few other people proofread your resume so that you can ensure it all makes sense and is well laid out.

Chapter 4 - Resume Tips

There is so much that goes into writing a great resume and I want to give you all the information I can, so in this chapter, I want to give you some resume writing tips that will ensure your resume stands out from the rest.

1. Use white paper to print your resume on. So many times, people think that if they have brightly colored paper their resume will stand out, but you have to remember that your reader is going to be looking at hundreds of resumes and if the paper makes yours hard to read, it is likely that it will get thrown in the trash.

2. If you are printing off your resume, make sure that you use a good printer that is not low on ink. If you do not have a good printer, you can use one at your local library to ensure that the resume looks as good as it possibly can. You do not want to hand out resumes that were printed on a low-quality printer or that were printed on a printer that was running out of ink because it will only make it harder for the reader to see and that means they will likely pass it over.

3. List all of the positions you held while working at different companies. For example, if you started working at a company 10 years ago as a laborer and worked your way up to floor manager, you need to list all of the positions

you held and what you did in each position. This will allow the potential employer to understand all of the skills you developed while you were in the company.

4. Do not list your reason for leaving the companies you previously worked at. If the potential employer wants to know, let them ask you during the interview and even then, make sure you put a positive swing on it. Remember when we talked about keeping the resume positive? You do not want to put on your resume that you left your job because your boss was a jerk because it makes you look like you are not able to get along with others. Instead, let them ask you and simply state that you were looking for more opportunities to advance. They don't need to know every detail.

5. Do not use the words "I" or "Me" when you are writing your resume. The reader already knows that this is your resume and that it is talking about you. Using these pronouns is just going to make you sound redundant. Instead of saying "I was in charge of new employee safety training", say "Responsible for the safety training of new employees". This will come as a bullet point under the job description.

Let's look at an example of this so that you understand better how you should list each job. We will take an example of a factory worker.

XYZ Company from October 4, 2000-August 15, 2011:

- Responsible for new employee safety training
- In charge of weekly safety meetings
- Line lead
- Implemented company newsletter

Do you see how the name of the company and how long you worked there stands out? Do you see how easy it is for a potential employer to scan down the bullet points and see your skills as well as what you were responsible for?

Do you notice that each bullet point does not start out with 'I was'? Remember, they already know this resume is about your work experience, so you don't need to keep reminding them. Keep it simple, keep it short.

1. Don't forget the basics when it comes to writing your resume. The first thing centered and in bold on the top of the resume should be your name. Under that, in regular text, should be your contact information. If your resume is more than one page (it should never be more than 2), you need to ensure that this contact information is on the top of both pages. If one of the pages were to get lost, you want to make sure the potential employer does not match it up with the wrong resume.

2. Focus on your accomplishments. Many people think that they should simply create a list of their job duties, but you should focus more on your accomplishments. If you are like me, you have more duties at your job than you want to list on paper and more than any future employer wants to read about. Save all of that for the interview and focus on what you have accomplished at each job. For example, if you started out as a laborer and worked your way up to management, that would be an accomplishment, but it does not have to be that drastic. You can list your small accomplishments, too, such as training other employees.

3. Make sure that your resume shows the skills you have that you *enjoy*. Just because you are able to do something does not mean that you are going to want to do it every day for however long you are with the company. If you don't enjoy doing something, do not place it on your resume.

4. Ask yourself these questions before you begin writing: Who am I professionally, what skills do I have, and what value will I offer. Once you know the answer to these three questions, you will know how you want to lay out your resume.

5. Get rid of the fluff. You want your resume to stand out, to grab the reader's attention, not cause them to roll their eyes because it contains all of the same information as other resumes. What I am talking about is stuff like "team player" or "excellent communication skills". These are things that everyone puts on their resume and it is nothing more than fluff. A filler for those who do not have enough

skills to actually fill in an entire resume and hiring managers know that. Get rid of it and use that space for actual information that is relevant to the job.

6. Stay away from resume templates. Yes, it may be tempting to run to a resume template, it may feel safe knowing that you will be able to fill in the blanks, but it is not going to get the attention of the reader. They will see just another plain resume, not something that stands out from the rest. Take the time needed to create your own resume. However, it is okay to look at a resume template to give yourself some fresh ideas, but don't go with a cookie-cutter resume.

7. Remember, a resume is a marketing tool and you are the product. When you are writing your resume, write it as if you are trying to sell something.

Those are just a few tips I have for you. Much more will be covered throughout the rest of the book, but I think it is important for these to be listed because they are so important to your success.

In the next chapter, I am going to show you what you should avoid doing on your resume by going over common mistakes. It is a great idea to go over these after your first draft of your resume is completed because you will be able to recognize if you have made any of these mistakes and fix them before the hiring manager sees them.

Chapter 5 - Resume Mistakes to Avoid

In this chapter, I want to cover all of the things that you want to avoid doing when you are creating your resume. These are very common mistakes, so when you are going over your resume, if you find any of these mistakes, don't feel bad because most of us make at least one of them. Simply fix your mistake so that the hiring manager is not the one who finds the mistakes.

1. Not proofreading your resume. No matter how focused you are, how well you type, or how much attention you pay, you need to proofread your resume. Even if you think you did not make any mistakes, you would be surprised at what you will find. There are free programs online that you can use to make sure everything is grammatically correct and make sure you check all of the spelling. For example, typing "than" instead of "then" could easily cost you an interview. To avoid mistakes, use these tips:

2. Do not use words that you do not use on a regular basis. Trying to sound like you know what you are talking about can do more harm than good when you are not using the words properly.

3. Use a dictionary while you are writing your resume. There is also a feature in Word that allows you to highlight the word, then right click on it, and see the definition.

4. Always perform a spell and grammar check when you have

finished writing your document. Most of us think that we can catch the mistakes on our own, but that is just not true. Because we do have these tools, it is important for you to use them.

5. Read every word of your resume carefully. This is where you will find mistakes such as typing "form" instead of "from". Not catching this could cost you the interview. Spell check will not catch this, and only some grammar programs will, but it is still important for you to read your resume word for word.

6. Check your punctuation. Make sure that there is a period at the end of every sentence, that you used commas appropriately, and that you did not use other punctuation inappropriately. Avoid exclamation marks on a resume.

7. Do not switch which tense you are writing in while you are working on your resume. This is confusing and will likely get your resume skipped over.

8. When you are expressing a number, you need to make sure that you are writing out all numbers nine and below (unless creating a numbered list) and using numerals for 10 and above. Make sure this is consistent throughout the entire resume. If you are beginning a sentence with a number, you need to spell it out. Example: Fifteen service awards, not 15 service awards.

9. Check for word usage. Common mistakes are "than" or "then", "except" or "accept", "affect" or "effect". You get the picture. Make sure you are using the correct word (this is why a grammar check is important).

10. Check all of the contact information for each job listed as well as the dates of employment.

11. Make sure your spacing is consistent.

1. Not including keywords that match the job description or post. We discussed including field related keywords, but you also need to make sure that these keywords match the job description as well. Often times, employers will give you a complete list of what they are looking for but people tend to not use those words in their resume. This is a mistake.

2. Make sure that your resume is up-to-date. If you do not

have an up-to-date resume, it is going to make you look as if what you have to offer is obsolete. One thing I have found is that many people will think that they did not get an interview because they were over 50 but when I look at their resume, it looks as if it is over 50 as well. Make sure you are listing all of the information needed and using all of the tips I have given you in this book.

3. Including too much information. We discussed earlier how it is important that you only include relevant information and you need to check this when you are proofreading because it is a common mistake. No one needs to know that you cleaned the company bathrooms once a week and took the garbage out in the break room. Remember, relevancy is key.

4. Creating an objective statement that does not match the job description. I think that the objective statement should be discarded altogether and explained that in a previous chapter, but if you are going to use an objective statement, you need to make sure that it matches the job you are applying for. Each job or field will have a different objective statement.

5. Listing position information that does not highlight what you accomplished when in that position. Anyone can say that they were the front desk receptionist, but you need to highlight what your accomplishments were. Maybe you were able to transcribe recordings of meetings for the company, which saved them from having to outsource the job, saving them 500 dollars a week. Highlight that, don't highlight that you can answer a phone.

6. Being too modest. This is another huge mistake many people make. They don't want to look as if they are bragging or they think that anyone could have accomplished what they did. That is not what is going to get you hired. Humility is a virtue and many companies like for their employees to display humility, but that does not mean you need to let it cost you an opportunity for an interview. This is the time that you need to build yourself up. Remember, you are selling a product and you are that product.

7. Creating a one-size-fits-all resume. I also talked about how important it is for you to create one resume for each field that you will be applying in. Personally, I don't think it is too much to ask to have a special resume for each job. You can have all of your information in a basic word document, then, as you are choosing which jobs to apply for, take the time to create a resume specific to that job. Some may be the same and some may not, but do not attempt the one-size-fits-all resume. It will make you look lazy to the potential employer.

8. Cutting things too short. I talked about how it is important for you to try to keep your resume to 1 to 2 pages, but don't sell yourself short just to stay within that 1-page resume guideline. I still don't suggest that you go over 2 pages. If necessary, change your font size to a 10 or 11 point but don't sell yourself short.

9. Not using action words. Instead of saying "Responsible for training new employees in safety regulations", try "Ensured all new employees were trained in safety regulations." This shows action. Something you did or were responsible for, simply states that it was something you were supposed to do.

10. Being too wordy. Remember, you are not writing a book and you are not trying to tell the reader your life story. You are trying to get the potential employer to see the facts that show how great of an employee you could be and that you would be an asset to the company. Keep it simple.

11. Listing jobs, titles, and contact information without giving any detail about your accomplishments. Of course, potential employers want to know what company you worked at, your job title, and how to contact them, but they want to know what you did. What did you do at the company that made you valuable? We discussed how important it is that you do not give out too much information, but it is also just as important that you ensure you are not giving out too little information.

12. Having huge gaps of employment. It is perfectly fine that you decided to take off for 5 years after you had a baby.

People understand that you want to be home with your child. Did you do anything during that time? Maybe you babysat or ran a small business out of your home. List that. If you didn't, simply state that. The way you would do this is: 2000-2005 (had a baby and stayed home until he/she started school. Sold Avon during that time). Something simple that shows you did not fall off the face of the planet for 5 years.

13. Trying to hide job hopping. This is a big one and many companies catch on pretty quickly. If you worked two or three temporary jobs, list them, but define them as seasonal or temporary. Maybe you had several part-time jobs at the same time. Make sure that is understood so that you do not look like someone who hops from one job to another. If you do come across as a job hopper, you will be seen as a risk. Companies do not want to invest the time that it takes to train you if you are not going to stick around. This just costs them money in the long run.

14. Not providing the correct contact information (most importantly, email information).This is the most common mistake that people make when creating their resume. Today, most resumes are sent via email and you need to make sure that you include your email address at the top of your resume as well as a current cell phone number. You need to double check your email address and make sure that you are not using your work email address. You may want to set up a new email account to use when sending out resumes because if you still have the email account that you opened when you were 16, it may not look that great to an employer. For example, a friend of mine's email used to be shannonrocks420_6tynine.This is not the type of address you want to send to a potential employer. Instead, try something like john.doe@email.com

It's all in the details when it comes to resume writing and even if you have to go over your resume three or four times before you have it perfected, that is perfectly okay. Make sure you have the small details handled and the big stuff will come together for you.

If you follow the tips I have given you in this book, you will have a winning resume and it will help you to get the interview you want. Not following these tips could cost you the job of your dreams so take the time that is needed to ensure you have the perfect resume.

STEVE WILLIAMS

Chapter 6 – A Quality Resume VS a Bad Resume

I want to begin this chapter by looking at a bad resume, we will discuss the issues, then look at how the resume would look if it was a quality resume.

Jane Doe

Contact   information:
Janehotandsassy@email.com

Objective- Motivated business woman looking for a full-time career

Education-
Bachelor'sOf Business Administration, graduated 2012
High school. Graduated with honors

Work Experience-
A&B CPA- Intern

It was my job to review books for smaller companies.

Reason for leaving- Did not get along with the boss

Dr. Smiles (dentist office) – office assistant

I was in charge of answering the phone, setting appointments and filing forms that were required for each patient.

Reason for leaving- Became bored with the work

Flip a Burger- Cashier

I took orders, ran the cash register and filled orders. Was also in charge of keeping the front of the restaurant clean.

Reason for leaving- Found a better job

Special Requirements-

There are specific days that I do have to have off due to my religion, I also can only work between the hours of 8am and 4pm due to having a child. Overtime is not acceptable for me to work.

Hobbies and interests-

I am a very interesting person that enjoys getting out and enjoying nature. I love going for hikes, camping, and fishing as well as swimming in the summer. In the winter I enjoy staying close to home, sitting by the fire as well as creating many different types of crafts.

About Me-

Most of my friends would describe me as outgoing and easy to get along with. I am generally happy all of the time and do not miss work regularly. I am looking for a company that I can grow with. I want to work in a company that understands how important the employees really are.

Now that we have this resume, let's start taking it apart, beginning with the first line. Jane Doe has used several fonts while creating her resume in an attempt to make things look pretty and to catch the eye of the employer. However, this only makes the resume look unprofessional and disorganized. Instead, you should make sure that you are using one font and that it is a basic font. Lucida Grande, Times or Georgia are fine fonts for a resume.

The second line provides the contact information for Jane Doe. Janehotandsassy@email.com. This will definitely jump out to a potential employer and will ensure that Jane Doe is not considered for the job. This type of email makes Jane Doe look unprofessional and immature. Instead, she should have created an email address specifically for sending and receiving business information.

Line three starts with objectives, however, it again uses a fancy font instead of something simple which makes this very hard to read. The color of the font has also been changed in an attempt to get the reader's attention and as we have already discussed, this is a great way to get your resume thrown in the trash. Once you read the objective, you realize that this information really should be placed in a cover letter (which we will discuss later in this book) instead of on the resume.

Moving on to education, we can see that she has a bachelor's of business administration and that she graduated high school. First of all, unless you are applying for your first job, there is no need to put anything on your resume about high school unless you did something spectacular such as graduated 5 years early. Also, if you have a degree, it is given that you graduated high school this is simply unnecessary information.

Next, I want to look at work experience. Under each job, you should use bullet points to list what your responsibilities were. Again, there is no need to use the words 'My' or 'I' in this section. All of the responsibilities should be reworded. When it comes to the reason for leaving, these are best left out. Let the person interviewing you ask, but make sure you have a good reason. Becoming bored with the work is not a good reason, instead, put a positive spin on things.

The last job listed is pretty much pointless. If the interviewer wants to know if you had other jobs, then you can tell them about the Flip a Burger job. If they ask why it was left off of the resume, simply explain that you did not feel it pertained to the job you were applying for.

Special requirements is a section that many people get caught up in and should instead leave off. It does not matter if you have a disability, if you have a specific belief or if you are allergic to something, discuss this after the job has been offered to you, but be willing to budge, because most companies are not going to accommodate special requirements that do not pertain to a physical or mental disability. For example, making the office meat free because you are a vegetarian.

Hobbies and interests are pointless information. This could include something that you are proud of but leave it off of the resume. If the interviewer wants to know about your hobbies or interests, they will ask.

Finally, we move on to the about me section. I don't know how else to put this, but no one cares. They will interview you if they want to know about you. Do not waste precious space on your resume and the companies time with this unimportant information.

Now that we have gone through a bad resume, I want to show you what a good resume would look like.

Jane Doe

1234 Happy Street
Happy Town Middle America
1-222-555-1234
Jane.Doe@email.com

Education:

- Bachelor of Arts in Strategic Communication at Iowa State University
- Minor in Business Management

Job History

1. ABC Hotels- District Manager 2001-2016
- Responsible for ensuring all employees received the proper training.
- Ensured that all hotels were compliant with government regulations
- Increased the star rating from a 3-star hotel to a 5-star hotel.

1. Dr. Smile Dentist Office- 1998-2001
- Responsible for checking in patients as well as ensuring all paperwork was completed fully before the doctor saw the patients.
- Sat appointments for patients leaving the office as well as over the phone.
- In charge of communicating with patients over the phone.
- Ensured that all completed paperwork was filed properly.

Accomplishments

- In charge of the monthly community dinner, helping the community get together and get to know each other.
- Managing the weekly food distribution in the town that I live in.
- Started a soup kitchen in my home town, 5 years ago and it is still operating today.

As you can see, this resume is much better looking. The information is clear and concise, and it ensures the employer is going to be interested in meeting you and asking questions. Of course, because of space, this is an extremely short resume.

You could also add a section for qualifications as well as one for training, and so on depending on the specific job that you are applying to. All you have to do is to ensure that the information you are providing is relevant to the job.

As you can see with the second resume, there are not special fonts being used, nothing is highlighted, and everything is in black and white. Center the headings for each section, ensuring that the reader can tell the sections apart.

It is important for you to carefully select where you will use any bold, italics or underlining. These should be used to help direct the reader's eye to important information.

When you are discussing the jobs that you have done in the past, do not just focus on the description of the job. It is very easy for a potential employer to find out what a job description in,however if you highlight your accomplishments, you will be more likely to grab their attention.

As you list your previous jobs, start out with one or two bullet points discussing your responsibilities or the job description, use the other bullet points to focus on your accomplishments.

As you create these bullet points, ask yourself, what is the benefit of the potential employer knowing this specific fact about what you have done. The accomplishments that you list need to be unique, these should not be a list of something that someone else has done but honest accomplishments that you have done. You should also avoid using any generic job descriptions when you are talking about previous work experience.

What is the most common mistake that people make on a resume? Most often, people make the mistake of using jargon that is industry specific. Yes, it may make you seem like you know what you're talking about but is the client going to know what you are saying? Just as common is that many people make the mistake of making many general claims. A resume should be used to sell you to the potential employer, highlighting your skills and strengths instead of turning into a bio about you.

When you are listing your accomplishments, ask yourself what would have happened had you not accomplished 'X'.

I stated earlier in this book that you are going to need more than one resume and the reason for this is that you need to cater your resume to each specific industry. If you are applying for several different types of jobs, you need to make sure that you have a resume for each type of job and that each resume highlights your qualifications to work in that specific job type.

Always make sure that you are writing in complete sentences when you are writing your resume, except when you are listing your responsibilities and accomplishments at each job.

Make sure that you list dates for the companies that you worked for. Simply providing a list of companies that you worked for is not going to provide the potential employer with the information that they are looking for. You see, when looking at a resume, the potential employer will not only look at the time you spent with each previous company but they will look at the time in between jobs.

I mentioned earlier in this book that you need to be able to explain the time that you did not work between jobs and this is why. If you were involved with your child's school during this time, make sure that is understood, or if you volunteered during this time, communicate that as well.

You should also try to add numbers to your resume. For example, instead of stating, was in charge of safety training, you could say, was in charge of the safety training of 65 employees.

Or instead of saying reviewed, books for clients, you could say, reviewed 6 books per week for clients, each 100 thousand words in length, minimally. Other items you can include would be the number of customers you served each day, what your total weekly, monthly or yearly sales were, how much you saved the money or how much you earned the company with up sells.

Never lie on your resume. If you get caught lying on a resume, it can follow you for the rest of your life. It may be tempting to embellish when you are writing a resume or even flat out lie because many people think this will help them get a higher paying job, however, there is no chance that you will not get caught.

If the company does not find out when they are going over your resume by calling the companies you have listed, they are going to find out when you are hired and are unable to perform the tasks required for the job.

You need to understand that even though a company says they are looking for someone that has 3-5 years' experience, that is what they are looking for in an ideal candidate. This does not mean that if you have 2.5 years' experience, you should not apply for the job.

I NEED YOUR HELP

I really want to thank you again for reading this book. Hopefully you have liked it so far and have been receiving value from it. Lots of effort was put into making sure that it provides as much content as possible to you and that I cover as much as I can.

If you've found this book helpful, then I'd like to ask you a favor. Would you be kind enough to leave a review for it on Amazon? It would be greatly appreciated!

Chapter 7- Writing a Resume When You Lack Work Experience

You should never allow a lack of experience to stop you from applying for a job that you want. You have to remember that we all have had to start somewhere and companies are going to understand that if you are a recent graduate or if you are an entry-level applicant, you are not going to have a lot of work experience.

Many of us learn in high school that we need to start building up our work experience as soon as we can but it is quite difficult to go to school and work at the same time so this often gets put off until education has been completed.

This means that for those that are just entering the workforce, that are changing careers or that have been out of the workforce for a long time, there may be a lack of relevant experience.

This is where you will use an objective section. For example, if you are a high school graduate, you will want to create an objective around the skills that you used in high school. For example:

Hardworking high school grad, (3rd in class with 3.8 GPA) with extraordinary social skills and research skills. Looking to use my skills to fulfill (whatever position you are applying for) at (whatever company you are applying for. My ability to quickly learn new skills will allow me to become a productive employee at your company.

This is a great objective for a person that has just graduated high school and is looking to start a career because it shows that the applicant is able to learn quickly and is dedicated to what they do. Any grade point average above 3.0 should be mentioned and if you are in the top 10 of your class this should be mentioned as well.

The next section of the resume will focus on your education. This will include the school you attended, the classes that you took as they pertain to the job you are applying to for example perhaps you took a computer programming class and are trying to get in as an entry level programmer. You should also talk about the sports you were involved in because these will show you are dedicated and know how important it is to be a team player and the clubs that you were involved in. The clubs that you were in are going to allow the potential employer to understand what your interests are and how dedicated you are. You should also include any offices you held in said clubs such as President of the Future Business Leaders of America.

Ensure that you also include any awards or honors that you received, even awards such as perfect attendance are going to be important if you have no work experience because it is going to show the employer that it is not common for you to miss days. This is one thing that they would discuss with previous employers but since you do not have any, you have to show them you have good attendance. You can also include any publications that you have in this section as well.

When you focus on the education section of your resume, even when you do not have any past work experience you are going to be able to highlight your skills and qualities effectively as well as show your potential employer that you are an enthusiastic team player. When you include your GPA, awards, and classes that you took, you will show that you have good work ethic and be able to prove that you do have knowledge that pertains to the position.

One problem that many people face is that they were simply not active in school. In order to solve this issue, make sure that you focus more on the classes you took and your grades.

It may take some time and some brainstorming to really expand your education section and provide the employer with the information that you feel is relevant, it is very important to do if you do not have any work experience.

Next, you will want to create a section for achievements. While you were attending school, did you ever organize an event? Perhaps you presented a specific project and won a prize, or maybe you volunteered at the local food pantry or wrote articles for the school newspaper.

You can also include achievements outside of school for example, perhaps you worked with your church to raise money for the homeless community or sold candy bars door to door so that you could go on a missionary trip, or perhaps collected donations to be delivered to the reservations. All of these are amazing and important accomplishments that while they have nothing to do with school should be mentioned.

Anything that shows that you can be a leader, that you are able to organize, or that you able to resolve problems should be listed on your resume if you do not have any work experience. However, after you have had a job or two, this stuff us much less important.

When you follow the tips that you have learned in this chapter, it will not matter if you have on the job experience or not. By highlighting what you have done in the past, your accomplishments as well as your education, you are going to be able to show the potential employer that you are capable of doing the job you are applying for.

It is also important for you to understand that you are not the only person applying for these jobs so you should not expect to get every job that you apply to. However, this does not mean that you should give up. It is important to know that for about every 12 resumes you put in, you will only get 1 interview. For the unemployed person looking for a job, perfecting and getting your resume in front of the right people should be looked at as a full-time job.

This chapter has focused on how you can create a resume if you have no work experience. In the next chapter, we are going to discuss how to address disabilities.

Chapter 8 - How to Address Disabilities and Your Resume

According to a recent census, about 36 million people in the United States alone are considered disable to some degree. 15 percent of those that are disabled are unemployed according to the Office of Disability Employment and 13 million of these reports that they have struggled to find employment due to their disability.

These numbers suggest that a person with a disability may have a harder time finding a new job which means that their resume has to be almost perfect. In this chapter, I want to cover how you should address your disability and what you need to do to ensure that you do get the interview you are looking for.

The number one question that most people with a disability ask when they are creating their resume is if they should mention their disability.

In order to answer this question, we have to first understand that the companies that are being applied to are looking for someone that can do the job. Therefore, before you apply to any job, you need to be honest, and ask yourself if you can do the job. If you can honestly answer that question with a yes, and know that the disability that you have will not affect your performance on the job, there is no reason to mention it.

I said earlier that you should never mention your disability on your resume. This is because, while it is illegal for you to be discriminated against because of your disability, it will cause the person doing the hiring to begin to question if you are able to do the job. There is nothing that can be done about inaccurate preconceived notions about people with disabilities, however, you can show the person hiring that you are capable of doing the job first and then let them know you have a disability later.

There are three main reasons that you should wait to disclose that you have a disability if you disclose it at all. The first reason is that you are going to get fewer interviews. There is no getting around it, when a person discloses that they have a disability, they have a lower chance of securing an interview.

Your resume should sell you, not point out any reason for the potential employer to eliminate you from the possible employee pile. You have to make sure that you get the interview, and if leaving off that you suffer from a disability will do this, that is perfectly fine to do. You also want to make sure that there are no food smears, coffee stains, or anything else that would get your resume thrown into the reject pile. The third reason is that The Americans with Disabilities Act states that you do not have to disclose your disability. However, you do need to ensure that you are applying for work that you can do.

The only time that you should ever mention a disability on your resume is when it will help you get the job which does not happen often. However, there are exceptions to every rule and this exception would be if you are applying for a job that has been specifically created for those that have a disability or if it is related to the disability that you have for example, many places will hire someone with ADHD to help work with their clients that suffer from ADHD, showing them that they can relate to others and that they can function in the outside world. Of course, ADHD is just an example, there are many other disabilities both physically and mentally that can help you get a position such as this.

What about gaps in your employment that are related to your disability? If you have a large gap, 2 or more years, you are going to have to let the potential employer know what was going on. Personal time or health issues can quickly explain why you were not working during that time. However, you should try to find something to fill the gap such as volunteer work, furthering your education or other activities that you took part in during that time.

When you suffer from a disability you have to be very careful about what awards or achievements you place on your resume as it could reveal to the potential employer that you do have a disability, allowing them to ask more questions. For example, "Gold Medal at the 1999 Special Olympics" will easily tell your potential employer that you suffer from a disability. However, "Secretary at the American Cancer Society" does not imply that you have a disability.

If you have a visible disability, for example, impairments with your speech, hearing or a mobility disability) it is best if you let the potential employer know about it before the interview so that they are not surprised when they meet you. However, this is not always necessary. Many gurus believe that once you get that first interview, it doesn't matter if the disability is visible, you have the chance to put them at ease, letting them know you have the skills needed for the job and you are exactly what they are looking for.

You also have to consider if you are going need any special accommodations. If you know that you are going to need some type of accommodation for your disability, then ensure that you have solutions ready for your potential employer that will be in the interest of both of you.

One example of this might be that someone suffering from diabetes will need two 15 minute breaks in order to inject insulin and the person would also need to have access to the refrigerator. Ensure that you have some solution for the company, for example, if the company has 2 15 minute breaks and a 30-minute lunch break, you could offer to take your insulin during the breaks.

It is very important for you to know what type of equipment might be needed in order to accommodate you as well as where it can be obtained. Show that you are a team player from the very start.

You should use your resume to open the door, then if you feel that the company needs to know about your disability, let that come out during the interview. However, if there is no need for them to know, there is no need for you to tell

Chapter 9 - Cover Letters: When to Use Them

Many people believe that they do not need to use a cover letter when they are creating their resume however, there are times when a cover letter is very important. The fact is that if you want to be considered for most positions, you need to attach a cover letter to your resume. So, what is a cover letter? The cover letter is going to allow you to introduce yourself to a potential employer, it will allow you to explain why you are interested in working for the company, you can highlight some of your skills and request that you be given the opportunity to interview for the job.

It is important that you take great care when you are writing your cover letter, ensuring that it is not only impressive but effective as well. This is what is going to give your future potential employer their first impression of you.

For this reason, you need to make sure that you are not simply creating a list of accomplishments when it comes to your cover letter but that you are showing your potential future employer that you are able to communicate effectively.

It is also very important that you include the proper content in your cover letter, use the proper format as well as the proper tone which can vary depending on the position you are applying for as well as your own personality. You will want to ask as many people as you can if it is possible at all, to review a draft of your cover letter, and ask that they provide suggestions for future revisions. However, you want to ask people that know what they are talking about. Instead of asking your mom to look at your cover letter, consider asking someone that actually works in the field that you are applying to.

How are you supposed to know if the company you are applying to requires that you provide a cover letter? Simply following directions is the best thing that you can do. If a company requires you to send a cover letter, they will state it in the job posting. However, if you are confused and unsure if you should send a cover letter, it is always best to do so, instead of losing the chance at an interview because you didn't send one. On the other hand, if a company does not require a cover letter and you send one, it may set you ahead of the rest of the applicants, the cover letter may be just what your resume needs to stand out from the rest.

To finish up this chapter, I want to give you some tips when it comes to writing your cover letter. In the following chapter, we will go into more depth for cover letter writing to ensure you write the best cover letter for your resume.

1. Do not start your cover letter out with "To Whom It May Concern". This is a very old way of addressing letters; it also shows that you do not care enough about the communication to even look up the person's name that will be reading your cover letter. Instead, try to address the cover letter to the hiring manager or whoever is in charge of the hiring process at the particular company. Most of the time, you can find this person's name in the job listing. It will be the contact name that is on the listing if not, most of the time, the listing will state who the potential employee will be reporting to such, simply searching up the job title on LinkedIn will provide you with the name of the person you should be addressing.

2. However, if you have done all that you can do and you still are unable to find the name of the person that you should be addressing, you can use a generic addressee, such as "Hiring Manager." This should only be used if you have searched Google as well as LinkedIn thoroughly ensuring that the information is not readily available online.

3. You also need to ask yourself what you really want to do at the company. Every potential employer is going to want you to tell them WHY. Why do you want to work for that company? Why did you apply to that company? This answer should not have anything to do with money. Instead, you should use one or two sentences to exactly why you want to work at that specific company, make sure you do research, focus on press releases and learn about specific projects or clients that the company has at that time. It is your job to be very specific in explaining why you would be a great fit for that company.

4. Always make sure that the first sentence of your cover letter stands out. Most people are going to start out with some generic, line, that does not even need to be stated such as, "Attached you will find my resume for the position of Project Manager."

5. Instead, choose to start your cover letter out with something more creative such as a positive statement from a recent performance review or defining a specific problem and how with your skills it can be solved or even by dropping a name or two of a current employee. The point is to get the reader's attention.

6. In the middle of the cover letter, you will provide the meat. It is here that you will explain that you have the skills that the company is searching for. Be specific in this section, discuss specific skills, processes or procedures. Do not focus on your ability to communicate effectively, this should shine through the cover letter and not have to be told. Instead, focus on the technical stuff.

7. Finally, you use the last paragraph to thank the reader for their time, reiterate that you are interested in working for the company and thank the reader for considering you.

Writing a cover letter does not have to be difficult but it is important for you to focus on what you are doing, and ensure that you are putting your best foot forward. Just like your resume, a cover letter can make or break you. If you create a bad cover letter, it could cost you the interview but if you create an amazing interview, it may be what sets your resume apart from the rest.

Chapter 10- Do's and Don'ts of a Cover Letter

In the previous chapter, we talked about when you should include a cover letter with your resume. In this chapter, I want to discuss exactly how you can create a cover letter for your resume.

The first thing that you need to know when you are creating a cover letter is what you should include in it and you need to understand that your cover letter should be no more than 1-page long.

In this one-page cover letter, you will need to assess the needs of the company and match your skills to those needs, showing the company that you are exactly what they are looking for. This is where you will appeal to the company's self-interest.

It is also important for you to understand that you are going to have to create a cover letter for each job that you are applying for. Each cover letter needs to be tailored to each job, showing that you have researched the company, know what their needs are and know what you can offer the company.

The letter should be written in a mature tone but it should also be clear. Just like when you are writing your resume, you want the person reading the cover letter to be able to understand what you are talking about and you do not want to sound as if you are boasting about how smart you are.

Make sure that you do not write in blocks or walls, instead, break the cover letter up into paragraphs, avoid using jargon, and keep the cover letter positive. The tone should be conversational, it should show that you are enthusiastic about the job and that you are respectful of those reading the letter. Most importantly, the letter should ooze professionalism.

You should show some of your personality in the letter, however, you need to avoid making it sound like a sales letter. Do not try to oversell yourself, or make your cover letter sound like a gimmick you would find online. Instead, start fast, showing that you are highly interested in the job and attract the interest of the reader as quickly as possible.

Make sure that you have a main point, the rest of the cover letter should focus on that main point and all of the points should be in a logical sequence. You don't want the cover letter to jump around from one point to the next, none of them making any sense when looked at together.

Now that you know what your cover letter should contain, I want to take a little time to focus on a few common mistakes that many people make when they are writing their cover letters.

1. Do not state what you are lacking. You should never say anything about a lack of job experience or talk about something that you have never done when you are writing a cover letter. You need to remember that this is to emphasize your skills and ability within the company, not to tell them why they should not hire you. The cover letter needs to focus on your skill sets and sell them to the potential employer, if you instead focus on your weaknesses or what you have not done previously, it could cost you the interview.

2. Always make sure that you check the cover letter to ensure it contains the proper company name and information. Nothing is going to get your resume and cover letter thrown in the trash faster than having the wrong company name on it. Always make sure that you are turning the right cover letter into the correct company. I stated earlier that each company is going to require a different cover letter and turning the wrong ones into different companies is not going to get you a job or even an interview.

51

3. Never lie about your experience. We talked about this a bit when it came to writing your resume but the fact is that it is true when it comes to writing your cover letter as well. You should also never lie when it comes to the interview either. These lies will be found out and they will be found out quickly. If you don't have the experience you need to get the job, instead of lying, go out and get the experience.

4. Always make sure that you proofread your cover letters. Typos are so easy to overlook and they no matter how simple they are can cost you're your chances at an interview. Everyone makes mistakes when they are typing. I type 10 hours per day 5 days per week and still have to proofread all of my work for typos, so thinking that you won't make a mistake is just silly. First, you should turn on spell check. It is important for you to use but don't always rely on it. The same goes for grammar check., it is great to use but it does miss some mistakes. This means that you need to print out the cover letter and read every word of it from beginning to end making sure that there are no typos, misspelled words, or grammar issues before you send it to a company. Since your cover letter is what is going to make the first impression on a potential employer, you want to make sure that it makes a good impression.

5. Don't spend time explaining why you quit your last job. One of the worst things that a potential employee can do when it comes to their cover letter is to try to explain why they left their former job or why they want to leave their current one. It is almost like you are going on a first date and telling the other person, why you left your ex. The potential employer does not want to hear about your past, short of what skills you used in your jobs, instead, they want to know about now, today, and the future. They want to know what you can do to benefit their company and how you are going to become an asset.

6. Make sure you take the right approach. So many times people begin writing their cover letter with something like, "I think I would be a good fit for this job because..." The truth is, no one cares what you think about your skills and

qualifications, they know how to assess those on their own, instead, they want you to tell them what your qualifications are. This means that you should focus on listing the skills that you have which pertain to the position you are interesting in.

7. Don't use the cover letter to focus on yourself. The cover letter is about focusing on the company; the resume is about focusing on you. The worst cover letters are the ones that focus on the candidate, what they are looking for and what they want out of the company. Instead of focusing on what you want, you should focus on how you will fit in with the company, how you will contribute and how the company will benefit from having you there.

8. Never badmouth your previous boss. First of all, you should never say anything negative in your cover letter, and this includes anything about your previous employer. It is not uncommon for negative information such as calling a boss incompetent and unfair, will get dropped into the lines of a cover letter and it will cost people the chance at an interview. Once this negative information is spotted, the hiring manager or recruiter will not even look at the resume, so just keep your opinion of your previous employer to yourself.

9. Never include a head shot. I talked about this a bit when we discussed creating a resume but often times people think it is important for them to include a head shot when it comes to their cover letter. It is not. The potential employer does not care if you are photogenic, a potential employer cares if you have the skills to complete the work that they need completed, not what you look like.

10. Many people include an objective when they write their cover letter, this can be a mistake because if the hiring manager begins to read it and the objective of the cover letter is not in perfect alignment with the company's objective, they will throw the resume away and move on to the next candidate.

11. Make sure that you are not underselling yourself. It is odd to think that a potential employee would purposefully

undersell themselves when it comes to creating a resume, however, often times they will write something such as "You probably have many candidates that are much more qualified than me..." or something along that line. This is a self-defeating phrase if you do not feel that you are qualified for the job, why then would you even apply? Instead, the cover letter should focus on what you can offer the company, not how humble you can be.

12. Never use clichés. When you write that you are proactive or a team player or that you are even hardworking, you are not telling the hiring manager anything about your experiences. The fact is that anyone can use those words to describe themselves and they don't have to be true, however if you talk about your skills and experiences, the hiring manager will be able to determine if you are hardworking and if you will fit in with the company.

13. Make sure that you do not get too personal. This is one of the worst things that you can do when it comes to writing a cover letter. You do not need to tell the hiring manager that your husband left you after 15 years of marriage with three kids to care for and that you never got to go to school because you have spent your entire life focusing on raising your children. You do not need to tell them that you are part of a specific religion or that you agree with the left or right wings. This is far too much information and all of it is irrelevant when it comes to the job as well as the hiring process. Most people understand that these topics are off limits when it comes to applying for a job however, it does happen on occasion.

14. Make sure that you are not arrogant when writing your cover letter. It is great that you talk about your accomplishments and skills but a cover letter is not the place for you to boast about all that you have done in your life. You need to make sure that you are coming off as confident and not that you are coming off as arrogant in your cover letter. The best way to do this is to have someone proofread the cover letter before you give it to any company.

15. The final mistake that many people make is discussing

salary in their cover letter. There is a time and a place to talk about money and it is not on your resume or cover letter. No one is going to want to hire someone that is only concerned about the amount of money that can be made in a particular position. Instead, wait until the job has been offered to you to discuss money and benefits.

Now that you know when you should include a cover letter, what you should include in the cover letter as well as what you should not include, you are ready to learn how to write your cover letter. In the following chapter, that is exactly what you are going to learn.

Chapter 11- How to Write Your Cover Letter

Before you can write your cover letter, you need to prepare yourself. You can do this by asking yourself the following questions.

1. Who am I writing to, who is my audience, who will be reading the cover letter?
2. What is the objective of the cover letter?
3. What are the needs of the person that will be reading the cover letter?
4. What can I do to ensure that my objective is expressed while focusing on the needs of the person reading my cover letter?
5. What are the benefits that I am able to offer to the person reading my cover letter and how can I express them effectively?
6. What type of opening sentence is going to grab the reader's attention in a way that is positive and that will ensure they read beyond that first sentence?
7. How can I ensure that the reader is going to maintain interest in the cover letter?
8. What evidence do I have that I can present to the reader that will be of value?
9. How can I ensure that the cover letter is able to advertise my resume?
10. What type of closing sentence can I write that will ensure

the reader will understand my skills and capabilities while persuading the reader to contact me for more information?

Once you have asked yourself these questions, you are ready to start writing your cover letter. There are many different formats that you can use but it is best to use a simple format that is easy to read and that pulls the reader's eye down the page just like your resume does.

You need to understand that even if your resume is not up to par if you write a great cover letter, that can be what gets you in the door and gets you the interview you are looking for.

At the top of your resume, you want to include your name, and contact information, just as you did on your resume. This should be centered, your name in bold and just a bit larger than the rest of the information.

After you have provided your contact information, you want to include the companies contact information, aligned to the left of the page. Start with the date, then the hiring managers name, followed by the company address, email, and phone number.

Next, you want to address the person you are writing to with Dear (hiring managers name) then you will begin your cover letter.

Begin by talking a little about yourself. Talk about the position you are applying for as well as how you found out about the opening at the company. Discuss your degree, experience or expertise. This will be the first paragraph of your cover letter.

The second paragraph is going to be where you sell yourself to the company. Talk about your previous work, your skills, your abilities and how you will be able to meet the needs of the company. Include phrases and words that are found in the job description in this section of your cover letter.

If you have done the research that I explained should be done previously, you will use the third paragraph to show that you understand exactly what is going on with the company right now, that you will help the company move forward and that you are going to fit into the company.

The final paragraph will be the conclusion. This is where you will create a call to action, explain that you would love to have an interview and that if you do not hear from them you will contact them in (however many days). You will also thank them for their time as well as the opportunity to work with the company.

That is it. That is all that there is to writing a good cover letter. You see it is important, just as it is when you are writing a resume, that you stick to the facts. Your writing needs to be clear and easy to understand. The fact is that most hiring managers are going to skim your cover letter and resume for about 30 seconds before tossing it to the side. However, when you follow the information that you have learned thus far and will continue to learn throughout this book, you will find that your resume and cover letters are catching the attention of the hiring manager which means you will be getting more interviews.

To finish up this chapter, I want to give you some tips to ensure that you are writing a great cover letter.

1. Make sure that when you are writing your cover letter that you are not just regurgitating your resume. For example, if you were to write, implemented company newsletter featuring employees on your resume, you might write something like, by implementing the company newsletter and interviewing employees I was able to raise moral by finding out what they needed to make their jobs easier. You see, when you are writing your resume, you are usually using bullet points describing your duties and achievements but when you write the cover letter, you are able to use full sentences, therefore providing more in-depth information about what you accomplished.

2. Focus on what you can do for the company, not what the company can do for you. The fact is that the company really doesn't care what you expect of them. They are going to offer you a specific salary, with specific benefits what they want to know is that they are hiring the person that is most deserving of that salary and benefits, the person that will provide the company with the most benefits.

3. When you are writing your cover letter you need to make sure that you are showcasing what you are capable of doing. When you explain what you have done in the past, hiring managers might become interested but when you begin what you can do in the future, for their company,

interest is guaranteed. You may even choose to include a paragraph that talks about what you can deliver if you are given the position. This will allow you to focus on your strengths as they pertain to the job.

4. The cover letter should be used to showcase your skills. Even if you know that you can do the job, maybe your past experience does not show that. Focus on your skills in the cover letter instead of the jobs that you had in the past, showing that you are able to do the job you are applying for.

5. You should not focus on your education when you are writing a cover letter. Your education is going to be listed on your resume, this is very easy to find on a resume and you should not use the limited space on the cover letter to repeat the same information.

6. Use the cover letter to tell a story. What was it that made you want to work with that specific company? Maybe one of the products that the company made, had some impact on your life, or maybe when you were a child your parents would drive by and you would always dream about working there some day. People love stories and stories keep people's attention. Just remember not to over share.

7. You should make sure that your cover letter does not sound too formal. No one wants to hire a robot. Instead, make sure that the cover letter conveys who you really are, friendly and approachable yet professional as well.

8. Remember, one size does not fit all when it comes to a cover letter. Each cover letter should be personalized; they should not be some generic cover letter that does not focus on how you can benefit that specific company. Always write new cover letters for each job. You can use some of the information from other cover letters but make sure that each one focuses on the specific company that you are applying to.

9. If you are having a hard time getting started, consider looking at a few example cover letters to get your brain working in the proper direction. When you take a look at other cover letters, you want to make sure that you are

using cover letters that are written properly. We will go over a few example cover letters in the next chapter.

10. Use your resume to show that you are real, normal and cut all of the fluff out. You don't want to sound as if you are making up a bunch of achievements, and you don't want to sound like some abnormal person that enjoys nothing but working all of the time, just be yourself when you are writing. After all, when you are not yourself on your cover letter, the company will see the true you when you are called for an interview. Getting the fluff out is very important because you have limited space when it comes to your cover letter, keep it short and keep it simple.

Now that you know how to create a cover letter and have all of the information that you need to ensure that you are able to create an amazing cover letter, I want to show you a few examples of well-written cover letters.

Chapter 12- Cover Letter Examples

Jane Doe

1234 fair street
Simple Town, Any State
Jane.Doe@email.com

Jon Bob, Hiring Manager
ABC company
987 Company Rd
Simple Town, Any State
123-456-7890

Dear Jon Bob,

It is with abundant enthusiasm that I am submitting my application for Safety Coordinator with your company. As a Safety Coordinator with over 15 years of experience, I am sure that my skills, achievements, and qualifications will make me an asset to the company as well as the entire team.

I have built my career in a variety of industries, while focusing on the safety of the employees. Each company small which not only allowed me to focus on the safety of the employees but also allowed me to work on bookkeeping, as a gatekeeper and take part in many of the company employee driven teams such as the Market Based Management team.

Not only am I used to having an abundance of responsibilities but it is something that I thoroughly enjoy. Having the ability to wear many hats at previous companies has ensured that I am able to not only be flexible but responsive as well.

In my spare time, I work for a small publishing company, where I edit and proofread 200 pages per week, allowing me to use my eye for detail to help others, by ensuring books are not published with mistakes. I believe that I apply this same attention to detail in all of my work and in my previous company was able to save them over 1 million dollars in Safety violations by focusing on the details.

Finally, I want to let you know that I have been a huge ABC fan for my entire life, as my parents used to drive by when I was a child I would imagine myself one day working for the company.

In closing, I am very excited at the possibility of seeing my dreams come true and working for ABC and would love to have the opportunity to meet with you and talk more about the value that I can bring to your organization. Thank you for your consideration and I am looking forward to hearing from you.

Warmest Regards,
Jane Doe

This is an example of a great cover letter. It gets to the point, grabs the reader's attention and discusses what Jane Doe can bring to the company. It is very professional and shows that she is very excited about getting a chance to work in the company. Of course, this is an example and it could be expanded upon but it is important for you to remember that you should not have a cover letter more than 1-page long.

Finally, I want to show you an example of a bad cover letter.

Jane Doe

Janehotpantsdoe@email.com

Attention Hiring Manager:

To whom it may concern,

Attached you are going to find a copy of my resume. I am applying for the Safety Coordinator position at your company and although I have not been a Safety Coordinator, I was the Assistant Safety Coordinator at my previous job and feel that I can handle the job.

I began my career in safety 4 years ago when my husband left me with 2 small children to care for. Even though I had 2 small children I was able to work a 40 hour a week job and take care of them. Eventually, I was promoted to Assistant Safety Coordinator. I also took part in many of the teams that were in the company such as the Safety team, The Behavioral Based Safety Team, The Market Based Management Team and created the Company newsletter.

I am leaving the job because I am the only person that takes any responsibility and my boss is expecting far too much of me.

It is important for me to let you know that I cannot work overtime as I have already stated I have two children at home, this is another reason I am leaving my current job, there is too much over time. You should also be aware that I will have to take certain days off, due to having children in order to ensure they are able to get to their doctor appointments and other obligations.

I am currently earning 45,000 at my job and would expect to earn at least 60,000 as a Safety Coordinator with your company.

Thank you for taking the time to read my cover letter and look at my resume. I will be expecting a call from you.

Thank you,

Jane Doe

It is my hope that as you were reading through this second cover letter that you were able to quickly pick out the mistakes that were made. Of course, this is probably a bit worse than what the average person would write, something still tells me that many companies have seen resumes like this before.

The fact is that it may sound good as it is coming out, as you are typing it, it may sound to you as if you are the one in control of the situation and that you are showing the company how confident you are but the fact is you are simply showing the company that you cannot do the job and this is why it is so important for you to have someone read your cover letter and resume.

However, you have to be very selective when you are choosing who is going to proofread your cover letter and resume. I state before that you should ask someone in that specific field to proofread for you and not your mom or someone close in relation.

The reason for this is simply. Your mom has never read anything that you have written that she did not think was absolutely perfect. Your parents, siblings, grandparents and even spouses are not going to tell you the truth when it comes to proofreading anything you have written. It is their job to make you feel good about who you are, find someone that is going, to be honest. That is going to say, hey this is a terrible cover letter and you need to start over.

Finally, all of this work is for not if you are not prepared for the interview. Take the time needed to learn as much as you can about the company and the job that you are applying for. Make sure that when you go to your interview you look professional.

Start at the top of your head and work your way down all the way to your shoes. Did you know that if your shoes are not taken care of, it could literally cost you a job? All of this works leads up to one thing and one thing only. That is getting you in the door and getting you an interview in front of the hiring manager.

Many people think that once they have the interview the work is over, they don't worry about fixing their hair, trimming their beard or putting on makeup. They wear wrinkled clothes that are covered in lint or 40 years out of style to the interview and their shoes are covered in mud. You have to know the company that you are working for if you want to dress the part when it comes to the interview.

To conclude, you can get the resume perfect, you can get the cover letter perfect but don't let it end there. Make sure that when you walk into that interview you are exactly what they are expecting from the cover letter and resume that you turned into them.

Thank you again for reading this book!

Steve Williams

Related Reading

I have the perfect complement to this resume building book to further help you succeed in landing the job you want. Getting the interview simply isn't enough. You need to know exactly what to do and say during the process to guarantee you the job.

I highly recommend that you check out my book, *The Successful Interview – Why Should We Hire You?* It is available on Amazon in digital, paperback, and audio format.

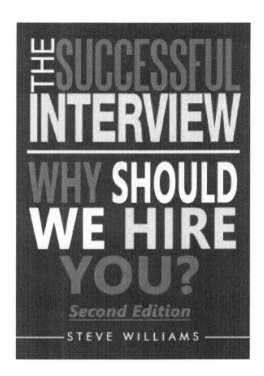

Go Here to View on Amazon:
https://www.amazon.com/dp/B011BCYED4/

Check Out My Other Books

Below, you'll find some of my other popular books on Amazon and Kindle. Simply search for the books below to check them out. Alternatively, you can visit my Author Page on Amazon to see my other works.

Go Here to Visit my Author Page:
http://www.amazon.com/Steve-Williams/e/B0125EAWUQ/

The Successful Interview – Why Should We Hire You?

The Winners Attitude – Learn How Winners Think to Achieve Success in Life

The Successful Leader – Maximize Your Potential and Lead Like You Were Born to!

The Successful Coach – Become the Coach Who Creates Champions

If the links do not work, for whatever reason, you can simply search for these titles on the Amazon website to find them.

LIKE THIS BOOK?

Check us out online or follow us on social media for exclusive deals and news on new releases!

 https://www.pinnaclepublish.com

 https://www.facebook.com/PinnaclePublishers/

 https://twitter.com/PinnaclePub

 https://www.instagram.com/pinnaclepublishers/

Made in the USA
Middletown, DE
29 September 2017